Book Intro

This book was written in memory of a man, also known as "Dad." He was not just any ordinary dad; he was the definition of a true family man. He was someone that never met a stranger and was a successful small business owner for over 35 years. As a child of a small business owner, growing up my upbringing was very unique and what I consider now to be very special. As an adult now with a family of my own, and a professional career of over 20 years working with small businesses; I wanted to share my story. A story of my dad and his journey, but also a self-help book for small business owners as they navigate starting, maintaining, and growing a business.

Throughout your reading, I hope you reflect on your purpose in life. Start by asking yourself a few questions. What is your purpose in life? What are your priorities in life? If you are a small business owner, why did you start a business? Maybe you took over a family-owned business, maybe it was to support your family financially, or maybe you were just looking for a work life balance with a flexible schedule. No matter your reasoning, I hope my story can remind you of your "why" and why you keep going each and every day.

People have always told me, you know how to tell a story, and you really know how to connect with people. I think back to those words, I get it honestly from my father. I also think isn't that why we are all here, to connect with one another. Dad's life purpose was to serve others, work hard, build and grow relationships, provide for his family, and have fun doing it!

I am the proud child of a small business owner. I hope you enjoy this reading and thank you for allowing me to connect with you.

Chapters

Chapter 1

A Simple Kind of Living

Dad also known as Pops, Mike, Big Daddy, Brother, Uncle Mike, Pawpaw, The Golden Boy, Mr. Randleman, and The Master Refinisher. He really was a man of many names. In this book I will refer to him as "Dad."

Dad grew up in a small town outside of High Point, North Carolina. From a young age, he was known for wearing a big smile, making people laugh, and a hard worker. He was raised beside a dairy farm, where he first learned the meaning of hard work. Dad would wake up bright and early before school to go milk the cows and feed the chickens. He would then walk back home and get ready for school. Dad was raised in the country and had a twang accent to match it, but he very much enjoyed the nicer and finer things in life. All the way down to his shoes! Family members still share stories of him loving to wear nice dress shoes to school. On rainy days to avoid getting them wet, he would simply put a grocery bag over his shoes until he got to school. By the way, nicer things to Dad didn't mean expensive things.

As a teenager Dad enjoyed sports and music. He was even in a band for a few years. The small boy band would play weekly at the local skating rink, where he would play the guitar and sing. Football was his favorite sport, and he played all through high school. His senior year of high school he was crowned Mr. Randleman. Teachers and classmates quoted him as being the class clown.

Throughout his life his biggest supporter was his mom, and the two of them had a special bond. Dad was one of four children, and was often referred to as "The Golden Boy." At the age of 2, his father died in an automobile accident. Even though there would be a few other father figures throughout his life, he always remained closest with his mom. Not really knowing his dad always weighed heavy on him. With the desire to help his mom and other siblings, he found himself wanting to be the provider and not depend on anyone else. His mom was a strong woman and a hard worker as well. She worked in a factory for many years while raising all of her children.

Dad held several jobs when he was young to make money. Even as a teenager, he quickly realized he had an entrepreneur mindset. At the age of 16, he took a job with a well-known interior designer, who also specialized in furniture. Dad found his passion for turning something old, into something new. He winded up being quite the artist. If any of you know anything about the High Point, NC area, it is also known for being the FURNITURE CAPITAL. After working in the trade for several years, he had a desire for moving somewhere different. He often wondered what else was there beyond the small town. He wanted ownership, to build a name for himself, and specialize in antique furniture. He knew he could turn something that may be considered junk to some, into memorable treasures.

Starting his own business went from being an idea, to a dream, and quickly his reality!

Chapter 2

The Mindset of a Young Entrepreneur

Dad was confident he could be successful with the skills he had learned. After a failed marriage at an early age, he decided to take ownership of his life. Taking the steps to start his own business, would give him the solitude he was looking for.

After just a few years, he was building a book of business and making a name for himself. In the meantime, he had moved to Salem, Virginia where he could stand out. In this town there was not much competition for this type of trade. He was growing a successful small business and then met the love of his life, also referenced throughout this book as "Mom." Dad and Mom were perfect for each other. They met at a bowling alley in the late 70's; both were in competitive bowling leagues. Story has it that he had long shaggy hair and a long beard. Mom's exact words were, "If you think you are going on a date with me, you better shave off that beard." As you would expect on that first date when he picked her up, the beard was gone.

In 1982 they got married, and knew right away they wanted children. He was the dreamer; she was the realist. Dad would run the day-to-day operations of his business; Mom helped with the bigger financial decisions and took care of his bookkeeping.

Dad had a history of spending money; money came in and money went out. Dad would often say "You have to spend money, to make money." Mom originally started her career in banking, and later worked in other steady nine to five jobs to provide stability and insurance for the family.

Dad would often say, "Antiques are like people, they all have a story behind them." Usually handed down by generations of families. Over time they tend to have wear and tear. Dad's goal was to keep the true character of the piece, and believed it was okay to make some repairs or upgrades along the way.

Some of you readers may be thinking, refinishing antique furniture is not a job many would seek out. And you're right, it's an art and for Dad it was a passion and his calling. God gave him this talent, to work with his hands. This trade allowed him to work independently, and generate lifelong relationships through his vendors and clients. Like other entrepreneurs, he didn't start the business to make millions of dollars. Dad got in to it for the solitude, to make an honest living, while enjoying what he did.

People think owning a business is easy, its actually one of the hardest things you can do in life. Most businesses that fail, do so in the first three years of creation. There is creating and starting a business, and then there is growing and maintaining a business. The maintaining and staying open is the hard part. At times being an entrepreneur means working long hours, and working extra hard just to survive. There may be times when the economy is so tough, you begin to ask yourself "why." The pressure is real, and you quickly realize the success of the business all depends on you. If you have a family and a business, kudos to you! You know first hand "Family" becomes your "Why."

Chapter 3

Realizing "Family" is the "Why"

Once married, Dad and Mom knew they wanted to start a family right away. Four years later they finally were blessed with their first child, it was a girl! And that girl was me, a child of a small business owner. Just a few years later, they tried again for another child. Unfortunately, they experienced a miscarriage. Then a miracle came just two years later, and a son was born. Now with a family of four complete by the early 90's, life seemed to be going well.

Having a family was everything to Dad. The business he had created, now had a new purpose. His passion turned into a necessity. The reality of providing for a family of four became real. When business is good and thriving, life is good. When business is down and things are slow, life can become difficult. Dad had the support of Mom, who played the role of keeping him grounded. This is also when his relationship with the Lord grew stronger.

Growing up Dad was always working. I recall his hands always being so rough, and he would apply lotion on them every day. Sometimes they would be so cracked they would bleed. He would proudly wear a t-shirt with his company logo, and a worn-out pair of blue jeans that he knew would get dirty. He would leave the house early for work in the mornings, but not until after he dropped me off at the bus stop for school. I have vivid memories of riding on his lap in his work van, and holding the steering wheel all the way to the bus stop every morning. We would sing songs and laugh as we went over the speed bumps in the trailer park. That's right, we were not rich by any means, but we were rich in love. Dad would say, "Baby girl we may live in this trailer park, but just know we have the nicest one in here; so be grateful for everything we have."

I didn't know what a trailer was. I knew I had everything I ever needed though; a roof over my head, food on the table, and a loving family. It was what we called home until I was around 10 years old. Some of my best memories were in that little home. I remember the wallpaper in the living room was an image of a bright beautiful sunset. We had one of those big boxed tv's in the house, which sat right in the middle of the living room. From the living room to the kitchen there were saloon doors that separated the two rooms. At one end of the home was Mom and Dad's bedroom, with what we considered the main bathroom. The other end, was my room that I shared with my brother. I don't know exactly how many square feet it had. However, when you are a kid; everything seems so big. I look back now and realize just how cramped we were. I remember the little old lady that lived behind us, and the one across the street.

When I got older Dad and Mom shared stories about certain things that had happened in that home. There was an attempted break-in, dad had heard and saw someone outside the bedroom window and ran outside with a knife to catch them. Lucky for that person, he never did find them. Another time my mom was sleeping with us kids in our bedroom, she thought she had heard something outside but drifted off to sleep. The next morning, they woke up to missing hubcaps from their car, someone had stollen them the night before. Again, none of this I remember or was even aware these events had happened. The things parents do to protect their children and their innocence.

Halloween was the best; everyone had their lights on and really got into the Halloween spirit of handing out candy. It was such a big deal, all of our cousins loved coming over to our neighborhood to rack up on the candy!

Every Sunday we would go to church. Mom helped with Sunday School, Vacation Bible School, plays, sang in the choir, and enjoyed cooking for the men's prayer breakfast. Dad would come when he could. Mom would remind him often; your children are watching you. This meant he was spending too much time at work on Sundays, when he knew he should be at church with his family. When he did come, he had the same routine and would sit on the same pew. The old chapel was so small. I remember me and my brother would count how many people were there. My brother was also known to crawl under the pews during prayer. Sometimes this even made Dad giggle, and then other times not so much. Cousins sitting nearby would often join in on the giggles, especially when Dad's belly would growl during prayer. The room was so quite we just knew others had heard. Dad's dress down attire during the week for work was not what he wore to church. Just like when he was a young boy, he always enjoyed occasions to get dressed up. Church was that type of occasion. "I got to get dressed up for the Lord," he would often say with his big smile. He would choose the brightest colored button-down shirt he could find. Bright purple or blue were his favorites, with matching ties to match. Final touches before leaving the house consisted of a quick spray of his favorite cologne, and slicking his hair back with his special brush.

Being a small business owner does have its perks, deciding his own hours and when to close up shop. When summer hit, he was prepared to close it up for some real family time. This also is when we would take our once-a-year family vacation. He would work long hours at night and on the weekends so we would have some extra spending money. We would always go on one family vacation a year, Dad and Mom made sure of it. We rotated mostly between Ocean Isle Beach, NC and Pigeon Forge, TN. When we would get to where we were staying, Dad would show us his cash in his wallet. He would say, "Now kids this is what we have for this week. When we are out, we are out. So, lets decide, what do we want to do?" This was one of my favorite qualities about my dad, his transparency. It didn't matter if it was personal or business matters, he always included the whole family.

Summer was a time of the year I looked forward to the most. School was out, which meant me and my brother got to go work with our dad! The days we couldn't go to his shop, we would go to our grandma's house. I tell people all the time, technically my first job was when I was 6 years old answering Dad's shop phone. The phone would ring, I would crawl up on a stool and answer "Hello, Wilkins Refinishing, how may I help you?" Over the years the customers looked forward to hearing my voice and getting to know me too. Dad would just laugh and smile as I handed the phone over to him.

He was always proud to have his kids in his shop. It was a different type of play yard. As you recall, dad specialized in refinishing antique furniture. This included stripping down the finish on the furniture, sanding, and staining a new coat. Some furniture needed repairs, maybe a new leg, new upholstery, or even replacing old piano keys. All of this required the right materials and tools. Paints and chemicals were all in the shop, as well as different types of wood, tools, and cans. I still remember the dust, wood chips galore, and the smell of his shop.

Dad preferred to sit on a five-gallon bucket, then a regular chair. Besides answering the phone, I would often help clean up the shop. My favorite was sweeping up the floors. Any money I would find he would let me keep. I also liked organizing his tools, and my favorite was the electric engraver. My brother and I would find small pieces of wood laying around the shop, plug in the engraver, and practice writing our names and leaving notes for dad in the wood.

The shop was located in a large commercial warehouse building with multiple units. It was shared with other small businesses. His unit was on the top level. I remember so many people we got to meet over the years. There was a rock band, an auto repair shop, tattoo parlor, food bank, and many more. It didn't matter the type of business; Dad would take the time to get to know each of them and always made a lasting connection.

Chapter 4

It's Not Always Easy

Remember I said earlier in the book, running a business is not always easy. You have to be confident within yourself and willing to take the chance.

Growing up Mom and Dad did a good job of not stressing in front of us kids about finances. However, as I got older it was hard not to hear the conversations. It made me realize his dream of owning his own business, may not have felt like a dream come true. He always found a way to keep going, constantly remembering his "why." He knew exactly how many jobs he would need, in order to make X dollars. As it got closer to vacation or holidays, he would then work his magic. He would work extra hard, buying, selling, trading, and at times took on bigger projects that meant working extra-long hours. I recall waking up early on Saturday mornings to go set up at the local flea market. This was a place Dad enjoyed going to, to make some extra money. This is when I got to see his people skills in action. He would greet each person like he knew them, and who knows maybe he did. Mom couldn't stand going, so between me and my brother we were always willing to be his sidekick. To this day, I still contribute my negotiating skills I have from my dad. I would watch him closely and was amazed how he knew exactly what to say to make a sale.

I would say you have to have GRIT to see success. That grit is what will get you through those tough times. Pick yourself back up, when you feel like you are down.

When I look back, Dad never knew the other resources that were out there for small business owners. The bank for example was a place that Dad just saw as a place that his money went in, and money went out. He never thought to meet with a business banker about his business account or loan needs. For the 35+ years Dad owned the business, he never once took out a business loan. All the financial struggles he went through, maybe could have been relieved or even eliminated had he had the right help and resources. My wrongful assumptions, I thought he knew and I thought his bank was talking to him and building those relationships.

I can't stress it enough, your relationship with your banker is right up there with having the right CPA and/or Financial Advisor. If you don't have one, get one!

Chapter 5

Relationships

Relationships are everything in life. When running a business, it is even more important. The relationships you have with your employees, customers, and vendors are so important. One of Dad's greatest strengths I've mentioned already, people skills. He never met a stranger, and could always find something to talk about with anyone. He was always genuinely interested in getting to know the person. He often made long lasting connections after just a few minutes with them. In running a business, this trait worked in his favor.

He did very little marketing to promote his business. He had t-shirts with his company logo and contact info printed on them. He also had business cards to hand out to new and existing customers. Then there was his van. On the back doors of his work van, he had his company name and contact information. Other than that, he didn't have to market his business. He didn't have a website; or any kind of social media. He didn't even have a computer system to manage his projects and clients. He had a rolodex at the shop, and used carbon copy paper for invoices and receipts. The top copy he kept for his records; the bottom went to the customer. Dad's favorite office supply, tape! He would label furniture in the shop with tape. The tape would have the person's name on it that the furniture belonged to. It all sounds organized, and I'm sure it was to Dad. However, if you were to walk into the shop on any given day; you would think hoarder. There was a method to his madness and he knew exactly where everything was. The repeat business of clients and word of mouth is how his business became so successful. When work was slow, he knew exactly who to call to ask for more work. When times were tough and bills had to be paid, he leaned into relationships to help him get through.

Vendors and supply companies he often bought materials from; knew he would always pay them but just didn't know exactly when. He always kept in good standings with them because he knew they had a business to run as well and respected that. The appreciation for one another went both ways.

Often times relationships came out of nowhere. I remember specific stories Dad would come home and share with us about his day. So many I could share in this book. First one that comes to mind was a young boy that lived across the street from Dad's shop. The shop was located in a rundown area of Roanoke, Virginia. Dad noticed a young boy always alone, walking up and down the street after getting off the bus from school. The boy would gaze over at Dad before going in his home. One day the boy came over to the shop and asked, "Sir, do you have any work for me? My parents are never home and I really need some money for food." Dad said "I'm sure I can find something for you son." Days and weeks went by, the boy would come over and sweep the floors and do other small tasks. Before you knew it, the boy had a new purpose. The smallest gesture meant the most to that little boy, and little did he know he meant the most to Dad. Dad's heart was filled with joy, just knowing he was helping him. Dad would often surprise him with a biscuit or a sandwich too, which always made both of them smile. They also shared the same interest in their selection of music. Dad would have his radio turned up loud as they both enjoyed listening and dancing to the oldies.

Unfortunately, the day came that the boy stopped coming and Dad later found out the family had moved away. You would have thought someone had died; the loss Dad had in his eyes when he told us. The worry as a father, that a child was out there in the world that didn't have food, structure, or a loving home. These moments are what reminded Dad to keep going and remain focused on his "why."

These types of stories always occurred at night, at the end of Mom and Dad's bed. My brother and I throughout our childhood could tell you some of our best stories, laughs, and memories were just having conversations about our day. Some nights I realized Mom would already be asleep, and there me and dad were just still talking away. I guess I got that honestly from him too.

All relationships, good or bad, always have a purpose and seem to make a lasting impression. Dad never forgot where he came from, that small-town country boy. He would tell me, "Don't let people know if you have a penny to your name, or a million dollars. Give as often as you can, and give even if you don't think you can."

During the week dad would wear clothes that were worn and teared, stained and discolored. He didn't care what others thought. He knew his worth, he knew what he could provide. He had customers come to his shop to pick up the furniture or to pay for a job, and often he found it comical to see their expressions of where the shop was located or what he was wearing. But again, Dad didn't care and those customers always came back for more. They saw the quality of his work; and realized those other things didn't seem to matter. Most of Dad's clients were financially well off and lived in million-dollar homes. Again, Dad never changed who he was for anyone, and always stayed true to himself. He looked homeless during the week, and looked like a million bucks on Sunday morning for church.

Then I remember a pivotal year, the day when our family of four moved. We moved from a single wide trailer in a trailer park with two bedrooms and one working bathroom; to a brick ranch style home with three bedrooms, two baths, and a basement. This new home was in a nice middle-class neighborhood, and you would have thought we had won the lottery. If Dad would've had a vision board, that one moment would have been on there for sure. Dad's vision board would have consisted of:

- ✓ Own a Business
- ✓ Have a Family
- ✓ Be a Home Owner
- ✓ Be Happy

The last one is what we all want in life. We all know pure happiness doesn't come from material things. You have to first choose to have joy and happiness in your life. Dad never taught us to be rich, he educated us to be happy. Always encouraged us to do what made us happy, and know money can't buy you happiness.

The Master Refinisher, this was a nickname given to Dad throughout his career. He always knew the risk when he took on a project to refinish a piece of furniture for a client. The good thing for his clients, he was a perfectionist. This meant at times he would redo a piece over and over, until the finished product was just right to present to the client.

You see Dad was in an industry where he was providing a product and a service. Delivering a perfect finished product, with excellent customer service. Dad had a lot of pride in what he did, and always had a desire to please. In my opinion these are character traits we should all strive for in life. Take ownership in what you do, enjoy what you do, and always put people first!

Chapter 6

Making the Connection

The year my father passed; I finally made the connection. Not only did I personally witness my father run a business, but I witnessed first hand what happens after a business closes.

When you realize your "why" in life, your perspective in life changes. It occurred to me; Dad was never alone. In fact, he always had the Lord right there beside him and guiding him all through life. It is an amazing feeling when you realize you are never alone.

The steps he took, didn't seem so big. The risk he took, didn't seem too scary. Starting a business, why not. The courage and confidence he had within had to have come from somewhere. Dad would often say when he was down or upset, "I wish I didn't care." He didn't really mean those words; it was his way of saying he was hurting inside. When you care, you open yourself up to potential hurt and pain. However, imagine if you didn't care, you would miss out on love and happiness. Dad had a big heart that the Lord gave him, and was not afraid to use it every day. Dad was often a rollercoaster of emotions, but it was all because he cared.

This was a time I took a deep look at my life, where I was personally and professionally. Like Dad, I too started a career at the young age of sixteen. I too had married young, and had recently gone through a divorce. One thing I was always confident in, was myself and my ability to work hard. I continued to work hard, but as a single mom and loosing my biggest supporter "Dad," I realized quickly everything I thought I knew about life was not true at all. Dad had made it look so easy growing up, but as an adult now I realized life is really hard. I had lived my whole life up until this point to make my parents happy, to please my employer, and anyone else around me. I realized I had left out the most important person, myself.

The year I loss Dad, was the year I found myself! That famous saying, "Stop and smell the roses." I did just that! I remember the loss and sadness I had, suddenly turned into hopefulness and happiness. My mind was filled with so many great memories and reminders that this place on earth is just temporary. One day I will see him again. My only daughter at the time, gave me a special meaning to life. I stared often, held her closer, read to her every night, and did everything I could to show her every day how special she was to me. Often, I would tell her stories of Dad, to somehow make it feel like he was still with us.

The last letter my dad wrote to me was on a scrap piece of paper. He had drove by my work and left it in my car door the morning of my 27th birthday. The letter read:

"Happy Birthday! Today was one of the happiest days of my life. A dad could not ask for a better daughter. And your daughter could never find a mother on earth better than you. We all love you very much and I hope you have a great birthday. Love you always, Dad."

Dad did thoughtful things like that all the time, not just for me but everyone he knew. He knew exactly how to make you feel special. I kept that letter in my car for many years. When I sold that car, I found the letter and held it tightly knowing yet again this was a sign Dad was looking over me and our family.

I learned to stay true to who I was, and did not seek out acceptance from others. I had found my confidence, independence, and lastly happiness. I was thriving in my career, not trying to be anyone else but me. When I went to work, it was never just to get a paycheck. It was to try my best, learn, grow, and help others. I later found the love of my life, and had two more children. I've learned when God closes one chapter, he opens another.

Professionally, I have grown into a thoughtful leader. I can get a job done, take on big projects, and hit goals. However, I always put people first and I never lose sight of that. No matter the titles within a business, we are all the same and equal. We all have lives outside of the workplace. Sometimes Corporate America makes it easy to get lost in the hustle and bustle of our careers. We must not forget we are all human, and we need to treat each other that way. I am proud to be bold and different. Even if at times I am misunderstood, I always appreciate the fact that I can just be me.

Dad once told me, "Baby you are going to be running that place one day, and you are going to be a CEO." I never knew what he meant by that. At the time of his passing, I had no desire and still don't to be a CEO of anything. However, as the years have gone on, I too have struggled with work life balance. I have been in the same industry all of my working career. I have worked in many roles, and over half of that in leadership. I think what Dad was saying, is he saw a little of himself in me. I too have always had an entrepreneur mindset, but just didn't understand it all until later in life. In my professional career, when I was leading programs, teams, or even projects, I always had something to say, opinions, and thoughts to give. In the back of my mind, I would say to myself "If I was running this, If I was in charge, If I had decisioning making authority, I would do…."

For someone looking to start a business or maybe you already own a business, have an honest conversation with yourself.

Ask yourself these questions:

- Are you the best version of yourself?
- Are you doing what you really want to be doing?
- What connections are you making with others?
- How can you live your best life?
- Do you have Joy?

Chapter 7

How to Start a Business

It starts with an idea or maybe a dream! Then writing it all down. This eventually will become part of your Business Plan. A Business Plan is like a cookbook of success, or a roadmap of how you will get there. It will outline what is your business, who is going to be running your business, and what is the succession planning. When you are ready to take the next steps, meet with a qualified CPA and Business Banker. Depending on the complexity of your business, you may also want to seek legal counsel. One will help you form the business and go over the tax requirements, the other will walk you through all the legal components to be aware of. Lastly, the business banker can help you with opening a business account and will be a great resource for you as you start, maintain, and grow your business.

Be honest with yourself during the early stages. You may not have all the skills to get started, so lean into relationships that can help you. Local communities have some great resources. Some can even help you write your Business Plan, and of course the internet is always a great resource to help you get started. Others can connect you with other small businesses to see how they thrive.

Chapter 8

Important Business Documents

There are important business documents you should have when owning a business. Below are examples of some important documents.

- Business Plan
- Business Licenses "If applicable"
- Copy of the IRS letter issuing the Business TIN# "If applicable"
- Active Status with the State Corporation Commission
- Operating Agreement "If a Limited Liability Company"
- Partnership Agreement "If a Partnership Company"
- By-Laws "If a Corporation"

Below are some documents you may need when you open a business account, or apply for a business loan.

- Copies of your last three years' worth of personal tax returns "for each owner"
- Completed and Signed Personal Financial Statement "for each owner"

- Copies of your last three years' worth of business tax returns
- Business Debt Schedule "a list of existing business debt"
- Copy of Operating agreement, Partnership agreement, or By-laws "the one applicable to the type of business entity"
- Most current balance sheet and income statement for the business
- Rent Roll or Schedule, Copies of Lease Agreements "if you own rental property and generating rental income"

Of course, any financial institution has the right to ask for additional items. However, this gives you a good foundation of what to have ready when you meet with the banker for the first time.

Chapter 9

A Business Banker is your BFF

Finding the right banker for you is so important. You can always start with your local bank; the one you already have a personal account or loan with. If they cannot help you with your business needs, they know someone that can and will be happy to refer you over to the right hands. A business banker or lender is going to want to meet with you. That initial meeting is kind of like an interview, or a meet and greet. This is an opportunity for them to find out more about you and your business.

- How did you get started?
- When did you get started?
- What type of business do you have?
- Who are the owners?
- What are your business account needs?
- Do you have any business loan needs?

A business banker is your best friend forever. Basically, anything you ever need throughout the life of your business you can call your business banker. They are also referred to as Relationship Managers. They are there to help you; when you are starting, growing, or simply maintaining your business. At any stage of your business where there are changes, you would want to call your banker and let them know. This could affect your account or loans you have with them. Examples include; major financial changes, possible late payments on a loan, change of ownership of the business, closure of the business, death of an owner, etc. It is always best to call them first and be proactive, before they are calling you concerned.

Chapter 10

The Ups and Downs

Throughout my banking career, I have worked with different types of businesses and owners. Small and large, new and existing, and they all have had their fair share of ups and downs. One thing I notice when I meet with a business owner for the first time, they love to share their story. How they got started, where they are, and what is the vision for the future. Another word that comes up often in the conversation 99% of the time, FAMILY.

Again, having the right connections and resources is what will help you get through those tough times. Don't be afraid to pick up the phone and call on your other resources. Your banker is there to help you as well. If you have business account needs or questions, call. If you have a loan and are concerned about not making the payments, call.

How you pay your personal debt; shows how you are going to pay your business debt. That means making sure you are keeping your personal credit report in good standings as well. Banks do not want to see collections or any late payments on loans. Make sure you are also managing any kind of credit card debt responsibly. This all shows that you are responsible enough to pay back any creditor that granted you a personal or business loan.

Chapter 11

What is your "WHY"

If you didn't know your "why" when you started reading this book, that is completely okay. Hopefully by now though you are starting to realize what is important to you. Below are more questions to ask yourself.

- What is your Why?
- What makes you happy?
- Do you want to be an entrepreneur?
- What are your strengths?
- What are your weaknesses?
- What relationships/resources do you have?
- How can I accomplish this dream?

Chapter 12

What's Next

Dad owned and personally ran his business for over 35+ years before passing away in 2013. The end was never a discussion. His sudden cancer diagnosis and death, surprised us all. Even leading up to his final days in the hospital, there was little mention of what to do with the business if something happened. This was an uncomfortable conversation, and one Dad was not willing to entertain. Once he passed, Mom was left with a lot to do. This included sadly closing down the business. Neither myself or my brother had the means or desire to continue what Dad had started. It was Dad's dream and passion, no one could ever replace him or do what he did. The loss of his business was equally as sad, to the loss of Dad.

My best advice, talk about these moments with your loved ones before this happens to you. I know it's uncomfortable to think about death, or maybe to think about your business potentially being closed. However, just know it's just as important as those discussions you had early on when starting a business. One thing we all know for sure, there is a beginning and an end to everything.

Have your wishes spelled out in your Business Plan, Operating Agreement, or By-Laws. Better yet spell it out in your Will too, or reference back to the business documents. The language should describe the operations and management of the business if something were to happen to the owner. Its always good to have it referenced in your personal and business legal documents. This is why all business owners, new or existing, should seek legal and financial advice. These professionals are skilled to help you at any phase of your business.

Final take aways; remember that anything you choose to do will have an effect on the world around you. Please think your way through and make thoughtful decisions. Rember, Family first and forever!

Author Bio

Bridgett Kidd is a wife, mother of three, banking professional, and now an author. She has a Business Management degree, and has worked in the banking industry for over 22 years. She was born and raised in Roanoke, Virginia. She enjoys spending time with her family, and travels often to the Tennessee mountains. Bridgett is passionate about helping and giving back to others. She serves as a volunteer for a local non-profit, where she is able to mentor entrepreneurs as they begin their small business journey.

Writing this book has been very therapeutic and a dream come true. This year marks the 10-year anniversary of the passing of her dad. The book started out as a journal, with pages of memories that could be shared with family and friends for years to come. Then it quickly morphed into so much more. A testimony for all entrepreneurs, and a story many could relate to.

Bridgett is proud of where she comes from. She has learned over the years to listen to that inner voice. It's okay to be different, think big, be bold, and embrace the entrepreneur mindset. She has so much appreciation and respect for others out there doing the same thing.

In Loving Memory

of

Mike E. Wilkins

1954-2013

"Wilkins Refinishing"

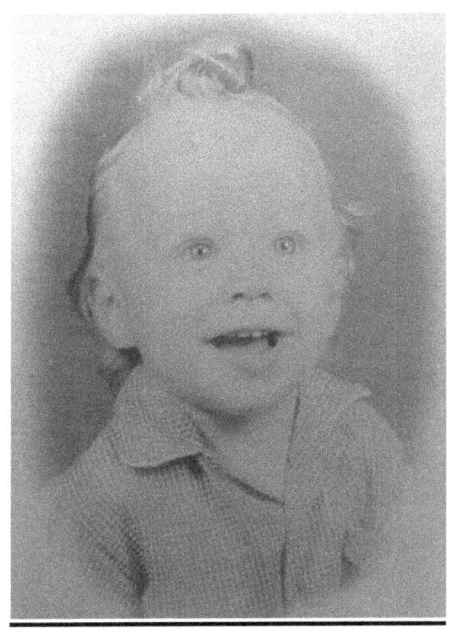